First World War
and Army of Occupation
War Diary
France, Belgium and Germany

1 DIVISION
1 Infantry Brigade
Scots Guards
1 Battalion
4 August 1914 - 3 August 1915

WO95/1263/2

The Naval & Military Press Ltd
www.nmarchive.com
Published in association with The National Archives

Published by

The Naval & Military Press Ltd

Unit 10 Ridgewood Industrial Park,

Uckfield, East Sussex,

TN22 5QE England

Tel: +44 (0) 1825 749494

www.naval-military-press.com

www.nmarchive.com

This diary has been reprinted in facsimile from the original. Any imperfections are inevitably reproduced and the quality may fall short of modern type and cartographic standards.

© **Crown Copyright**
Images reproduced by permission of The National Archives, London, England, 2015.

Contents

Document type	Place/Title	Date From	Date To
Heading	WO95/1263/2		
Heading	1st Division 1st Battalion Scots Guards 1914 Aug-1915 July To Guards Div		
Heading	1st Guards Brigade 1st Division 1st Battalion The Scots Guards August 1914		
War Diary	Aldershot	04/08/1914	13/08/1914
War Diary	The Continent	14/08/1914	01/09/1914
Heading	1st Guards Brigade. 1st Division.1st Battalion The Scots Guards September 1914		
War Diary		01/09/1914	20/10/1914
Heading	1st Guards Brigade 1st Division 1st Battalion The Scots Guards October 1914		
War Diary		28/09/1914	31/10/1914
Miscellaneous	Historical Section (Military Branch), Committee of Imperial Defence, 2, Cavendish Square. W.1.	20/09/1921	20/09/1921
Miscellaneous	Brackley Ballater, N.B.	23/09/1921	23/09/1921
Miscellaneous	Headquarters, Scots Guards Buckingham Gate, S.W.	27/09/1921	27/09/1921
Heading	1st Guards Brigade. 1st Guards Brigade, 1st Battalion The Scots Guards November 1914		
War Diary		01/11/1914	28/11/1914
Heading	1st Guards Brigade. 1st Division.1st Battalion The Scots Guards December 1914		
War Diary		17/11/1914	01/01/1915
Heading	1st Division 1st Brigade 1st Battalion Scots Guards Jan-July 1915		
Heading	1st Division 1st Bde War Diary 1st Scots Guards January 1915		
War Diary		01/01/1915	26/01/1915
Heading	1st Division 1st Bde War Diary 1st Scots Guards. February 1915		
War Diary		02/02/1915	05/03/1915
Heading	1st Division 1st Bde. War Diary 1st Scots Guards. March 1915		
War Diary		01/03/1915	05/04/1915
Heading	1st Infantry Brigade 1st Division. War Diary 1st Scots Guards. April 1915		
Miscellaneous	On His Majesty's Service.		
War Diary		01/04/1915	30/04/1915
Heading	1st Infantry Brigade 1st Division War Diary 1st Scots Guards. May 1915		
Miscellaneous	On His Majesty's Service.		
War Diary		01/05/1915	31/05/1915
Heading	1st Infantry Brigade. 1st Division War Diary 1st Scots Guards. June 1915		
Miscellaneous	On His Majesty's Service.		
War Diary		01/06/1915	30/06/1915
Heading	1st Infantry Brigade 1st Division War Diary 1st Scots Guards. July 1915 (1.7.15-3.8.15)		
War Diary	At Verquin	01/07/1915	03/07/1915
Miscellaneous	On His Majesty's Service.		

War Diary	At Verquin	01/07/1915	05/07/1915
War Diary	In trenches at Le Rutoire	06/07/1915	09/07/1915
War Diary	At Labourse	10/07/1915	12/07/1915
War Diary	In Trenches at Le Rutoire	13/07/1915	16/07/1915
War Diary	At Vermelles	17/07/1915	19/07/1915
War Diary	At Verquin	20/07/1915	25/07/1915
War Diary	In Trenches at Z 2	26/07/1915	28/07/1915
War Diary	In Bullets at Sailly Labourse	29/07/1915	31/07/1915
War Diary	In Trenches South of La Bassee	01/08/1915	03/08/1915

Mon 95 | 263 | 2

1ST DIVISION

1ST BATTALION SCOTS GUARDS

AUG – DEC 1914

14th Aug – 1915 July

To Guards Div

1st Guards Brigade.

1st Division.

1st BATTALION

THE SCOTS GUARDS

AUGUST 1914

Army Form C. 2118.

WAR DIARY
or
INTELLIGENCE SUMMARY.
(Erase heading not required.)

1ST BATTALION SCOTS GUARDS

Page 1

Hour, Date, Place 1914	Summary of Events and Information	Remarks and References to Appendices
Aldershot Aug 4th (6 p.m.)	Order to "mobilize" received.	
Aug 5th	Three fourths of Reservists arrived - magnificent clean steady men.	
6th	Completed to War Establishment.	
7th	Battalion complete in every detail and ready to move by midnight. Horses arrived early morning	
8th	Perfecting arrangements. Musketry practice and training for Reservists	
9th, 10th	As on 8th.	
11th	Brigade Route march	
12th	General instructions for embarkation issued	
13th	Entrained Farnboro' Stn. for Southampton in 2 trains. 1st left 5.3 a.m. arrived 6.45 a.m. 2nd left 6.25 a.m. arrived 8 a.m. Battn. complete, with vehicles (but without horses) entrained on S.S. "Dunvegan Castle". Sailing at 12 noon. Horses followed later in S.S. "Orange Prince".	

Army Form C. 2118.

2

WAR DIARY
or
INTELLIGENCE SUMMARY.
(Erase heading not required.)

Instructions regarding War Diaries and Intelligence Summaries are contained in F. S. Regs., Part II. and the Staff Manual respectively. Title pages will be prepared in manuscript.

Hour, Date, Place		Summary of Events and Information	Remarks and References to Appendices
The Continent.	Aug. 14th	Arrived Le Havre at about 1am. Disentrained and marched to Camp nr. Harfleur (6 miles) Stores which were left behind when Battalion Entrained arrived at about 11 a.m.	
	15th/16th	Left camp at Harfleur at 9pm for Lessaine Stn. Entrained by 4 a.m. & proceeded via Rouen Amiens Arras Cambrai to Le Touvin - billeted there the night	
	17th	Marched from Le Nouvion to Boué (4 miles) and billeted there. 2nd Guards Brigade Concentrated and came under orders of the Brigadier	
	18th	Billets Boué Brigade Route march (10 miles)	
	19th	- do - (9 miles)	
	20th	- do - (7 miles)	
	21st	Marched to Carlignies (10 miles) and billeted there	

Army Form C. 2118.

WAR DIARY
or
INTELLIGENCE SUMMARY.
(Erase heading not required.)

Hour, Date, Place	Summary of Events and Information	Remarks and References to Appendices
Aug 22nd	Marched at 2.30 a.m. by Dompierre. Halted for dinner nr Beaufort. At 4 pm ordered to billets at Limont Fontaine, but this was countermanded, and at 6 pm marched N. through Maubeuge and to billets at Grand Reng.	
Aug. 23rd	Arrived at Grand Reng (Belgium) at 1 a.m. — Stood to arms at 4.30 a.m.	
24th	Left at 4 a.m. to hold line of main road about 1½ miles to NE. On reaching this point received orders to move to a line W. of Villers Sire Nicole, and dug a line of deep trenches to resist expected move from N. At 5 p.m. moved off and marched till 10 p.m. to billets at La Longueville.	
25th	Left at 6.30 a.m. and went into billets at Taisnières at 3 p.m. — the Battalion being separated from the rest of the Brigade	
26th	Ready to leave at 5 a.m. but the road was blocked by British and French troops and therefore only left at 7.30 a.m. rejoining the Brigade (as reserve)	

WAR DIARY or INTELLIGENCE SUMMARY

(Erase heading not required.)

Army Form C. 2118.

Hour, Date, Place	Summary of Events and Information	Remarks and References to Appendices
	At a point 1½ miles W. of Le Grand Fayt. Early in the afternoon moved back and occupied a line W. of Evrurand to cover retirement of 3rd Bde. Marched as as rear guard to billet to Beaulieu. The men very exhausted and wet through before they got into billets at 10 p.m. Large numbers fell out but rejoined later.	
Aug 27.	Moved at 6 a.m. and dug a line of trenches evening from first in the E. of our billets to Wassigny, through F⁴ de l'Arbonnaire. Very heavy rain at noon, men trenched. At 2 p.m. If and C Coys dropped back to cover our retirement, and we arrived in Etreux to join the Brigade. A number of enemy's patrols E. of the town so B.& C. picketed road in that side till evening. We never moved on Guise, crossing high ground in artillery formation. Just before the 3rd C. reached the new road, enemy opened on us with F.A. Howitzers and infantry. The latter at long range died down and there was no difficulty in getting away. Aug 2 slight casualties. Went on through Guise to Jonqueure and bivouaced at 11 p.m. – men exhausted.	2 men wounded.

Army Form C. 2118.

WAR DIARY
OR
INTELLIGENCE SUMMARY.
(Erase heading not required.)

Instructions regarding War Diaries and Intelligence Summaries are contained in F. S. Regs., Part II. and the Staff Manual respectively. Title pages will be prepared in manuscript.

Hour, Date, Place	Summary of Events and Information	Remarks and References to Appendices
Aug 28st	Poured Down with difficulty and left at 4 a.m. a most trying march very hot, all Cavalry infested by the 2nd division. 1½ hr halt near Bicary for dinner helped us along and we reached St Gobain at dusk, with the loss of relatively few men	
" 29d	Stood to arms at 4.30 a.m. Soon after 6 a.m. a notification came that there was to be a day of rest	
" 30d	Paraded at 12.30 a.m. and marched till 8 a.m. to Terny to be Divnl. Reserve at Army H.Qrs. Bivouacced in field till 5 p.m. then moved to Allemont and bivouacced.	
" 31st	Moved 5 a.m. Paris-Maubeuge road at 8 a.m. Stopped N. of Siereus to repel of Prussian Cavalry. Coy marched through Crepy in steep hills to Feuillise and Duvinoches in field	
Sept 1st	Moved marched by 3.30 a.m. marched on through Crise Dominiele to R.B. Dinner at Villers Cotterets. Marched to La Ferte Milon on Pond du Marne. Took up position alone and St Gorin before dark Slept in Cornfield for few hours. Ministerial Convel on wagons specially provided.	

1st Guards Brigade.

1st Division.

1st BATTALION

THE SCOTS GUARDS.

SEPTEMBER 1 9 1 4

1st Scots Guards

Copied from last page of August War Diary

WAR DIARY

SEPTEMBER 1914

Sept. 1st	Wagons packed by 3.30 a.m. Marched 6 a.m. through FORET DOMINIALE de METZ. Dinners at VILLERS COTTERETS. Marched to LA FERTE MILON on Route de Meaux. Took up position above and S. of town before/dark, slept in cornfield for few hours. Men's packs carried on wagons specially provided.

WAR DIARY
or
INTELLIGENCE SUMMARY.
(Erase heading not required.)

Army Form C. 2118.

Hour, Date, Place	Summary of Events and Information	Remarks and References to Appendices
Sept 2nd	Started at 1.20 a.m. on the Meaux road, halted for breakfast at 7 a.m. Moved on at 10.45 a.m. to Chambrey arriving at 2.30 p.m. and billeted.	
" 3rd	Orders to reinforce outposts if necessary at short notice but not required. Paraded at 3.45 a.m. for rear guard and took up position on outpost line. Commence march at 7.20 a.m. crossing the R. Marne at Germigny. Stopped at 2 p.m. for dinners after having marched through Bois de Marré. Moved on to Jouarre and billeted in an old convent.	
" 4th	Marched at 4 a.m. to Coulommiers. Ready to march at 7 p.m. but move cancelled till next morning.	
" 5th	Marched at 4 a.m. to Rosoy. Battalion in Reserve. Lt Gordon Ives and 91 men arrived as reinforcement. Cavalry patrols bickered each company.	1st Reinforcement Lt Gordon Ives and 91 R and F
" 6th	Our Corps to move N.E. from Rosoy. Our outpost line relieved by 13th Brigade. Advanced guard of 15th Brigade checked ahead. Voulx and had to retire under heavy shell fire. Battalion advanced position on right rear of Brigade. General advance at 4.30 p.m. and met no opposition. Passed through Voulx to La Meure and bivouacked	

WAR DIARY or INTELLIGENCE SUMMARY.

(Erase heading not required.)

Army Form C. 2118.

Hour, Date, Place	Summary of Events and Information	Remarks and References to Appendices
Sept 7th	Marched at 10.35 a.m. to Amillis for divisions 2nd and 3rd Brigade in front by R.Aubertin and Choisy to La Ferris – Billeted.	
" 8th	Started at 6 a.m. short notice by Coury Sur Morin Church Martin Bellot where Brigade was shelled from question Villenouvre & marched in to Brigade Reserve outside Hoste Villiers Nogent Rd. Battalion on outpost about Breuteville With Coulay immediately in front – 4th Bn on left. G. Mercerton with regiments Shift of 93 joined the Battalion.	2nd Reinforcement. L:F.A. Henderson and 93 Rank F. 1 man wounded.
" 9th	Ready to move at 6.45 am but stayed north where Reveille was Marne Valley could move as ingest L'Artaux. Then by Charly sur Marne was at Crew Hill to Lafayward where halted for tea. On again at 2.30 pm to bivouac at La Moret. Rain from midnight.	
" 10th	Breakfast at 4.30 am. Start at 7 am still raining moving by La Thiolet Torcy Guichampa where 3rd Brigade was heavily engaged & mixed near Sommelans to about ½ hour. Marched at 3.15 pm to Latilly close by and billeted.	
" 11th	Breakfast at 4.30 am. Started at 5 am end by La Croix, Oumenlarieres, Neuilmil, to N.E. of Buzypers & Rolles. Rain in afternoon.	

WAR DIARY
or
INTELLIGENCE SUMMARY.

(Erase heading not required.)

Army Form C. 2118.

Hour, Date, Place	Summary of Events and Information	Remarks and References to Appendices
Sept. 12th	Breakfast at 5.30 a.m. more at 9am. by Fire in Bivouac to Soupigne to dinner. Move on at 4.30 pm by Bruys and Mont Notre Dame to Bazoches in pouring rain. One Company billeted, others bivouaced.	
" 13th	Breakfast 5.30 a.m. Crossed the Aisne at Bourg. Moved to Vegny above Bruilly and had the Town de Bruilly to Paissy where the Battalion billeted. Some casualties from long range artillery fire.	2nd Lt W.G. Hautsworth and 3 men killed Lt C.J. Balfour, 2/Lt G.V.F. Mosley and 11 men wounded
" 14th	Moved at 5.30 a.m. via Moulins & Vendresse to Chivy between that place and Troyon - 2 Companies in Brigade reserve and 2 Companies sent as Artillery escort to Troyon de Paissy	Major J.F. Green, Cpt. Carman, 2nd Lt H.R. Jones, 2nd Lt R.A. Compton Thornhill and 16 men killed. Lt G.M.C. Lowther, 2nd Lt E.D. Mackenzie, J. Stirling Stuart and 96 men wounded. 12 men missing.
" 15th - 19th	In trenches near VENDRESSE	
" 20th	To Billets at OEUILLY.	
" 21st	Left OEUILLY at 6 pm and relieved 6th Brigade in trenches near MOUSSY.	
" 22-23rd	In trenches near MOUSSY	
" 24th	Left MOUSSY for VERNEUIL and occupied trenches there	

Army Form C. 2118.

WAR DIARY
or
INTELLIGENCE SUMMARY.
(Erase heading not required.)

9

Hour, Date, Place	Summary of Events and Information	Remarks and References to Appendices
Sept. 25th	In trenches at VERNEUIL	1. 5/8
" 26th	Left VERNEUIL at 7.p.m marched to OEUILLY and went into billets there	
" 27th	Left billets at OEUILLY and marched to VENDRESSE reoccupying the trenches N. of that place.	
Sept. 28th to Oct. 15th	In trenches N of VENDRESSE.	Oct 9th 3rd Reinforcement. Lts Sir J.S. Dyer, A.W. Douglas Dick, J.L. Wickham and 50 R and F.
Oct 16th	Left trenches and marched to BLANZY into billets there	Total Casualties on the AISNE Killed Wounded Missing Officers 4 5 - Other Ranks 37 157 12
Oct 17th	Left billets at BLANZY marched [going] to FISMES and entrained there, leaving at 3.30 p.m.	
" 18th	Arrived at HAZEBROUCK detrained at 6 p.m and billetted there.	
" 19th	Billets at HAZEBROUCK	
" 20th	Left HAZEBROUCK at 9.a.m and marched to POPERINGHE to billets	

1st Guards Brigade.

1st Division.

1st BATTALION

THE SCOTS GUARDS

OCTOBER 1 9 1 4

copied from last page of September War Diary

WAR DIARY

Sept 28th to October 15th	In trenches N. of VENDRESSE Oct. 9th 3rd Reinforcement Lts.Sir.J.S.Dyer, A.T.Douglas Dick, J.L.Wickham & 50 R.& F. Total casualties on the AISNE K. W. M. Officers 4 5 - Other ranks 37 157 12
October 16th	Left trenches and marched to BLANZY going into billets there.
" 17th	Left billets at BLANZY, marched to FISMES and entrained there, leaving at 3.30 p.m.
18th	Arrived at HAZEBROUCK detrained at 6 p.m. and billetted there.
19th	Billets at HAZEBROUCK.
20th	Left HAZEBROUCK at 9 a.m. and marched to POPERINGHE to billets.

Army Form C. 2118.

10

WAR DIARY
or
INTELLIGENCE SUMMARY.
(*Erase heading not required.*)

Instructions regarding War Diaries and Intelligence Summaries are contained in F. S. Regs., Part II. and the Staff Manual respectively. Title pages will be prepared in manuscript.

Hour, Date, Place	Summary of Events and Information	Remarks and References to Appendices
Oct. 21st	Left POPERINGHE at 5.30 a.m. and advanced to attack Enemy N. of BOESINGHE in support of 4th A.C. Took up a line of trenches - Bang LF at KOEKUIT C and RF at BIXSCHOOTE. Find a Brigade of French Territorials between BIXSCHOOTE and canal, and several regiments of Cuirassiers.	1/S.F.
" 22nd	In trenches. French Territorials attack and try to turn Germans out of BIXSCHOOTE, but fail. They then retire to the other side of canal. Camerons, Black Watch and Cuirassiers heavily attacked, and Camerons lose their trenches.	2nd Lt. Mgr. Lawson killed. Lt. G.F. de Teissier wounded. App 1, 2 + 3
" 23rd	BIXSCHOOTE. 2nd Brigade counter attack & retake Cameron trenches, also 250 German prisoners. C Coy support their advance.	
" 24th	BIXSCHOOTE. Heavy shelling. Germans make a trench in front of BIXSCHOOTE, but are turned out by our guns leaving all their kit in the trenches.	Total casualties in the BIXSCHOOTE district. Killed Wounded Missing Officers 1 7 — Other ranks 8 25 5
" 25th	Left position at 12 midnight 24th/25th being relieved in the trenches by the French. Battalion turned night by roadside and marched to ZILLEBEKE S. of YPRES, going into billets.	

(9 20 6) W 3332—1107 103,000 10/13 H W V   Forms/C. 2118/10.

Army Form C. 2118.

WAR DIARY
or
INTELLIGENCE SUMMARY.
(Erase heading not required.)

Instructions regarding War Diaries and Intelligence
Summaries are contained in F. S. Regs., Part II.
and the Staff Manual respectively. Title pages
will be prepared in manuscript.

Hour, Date, Place	Summary of Events and Information	Remarks and References to Appendices
Oct 26th	Left ZILLEBEKE 5.30 a.m. and marched via HOOGE and reinforced firing line on L. of 2nd Division at GHELUVELT. Made an attack over very flat open ground towards POEZELHOEK but was held up by enemy's artillery and machine gun fire. Took over Bedford's trenches in the evening.	Killed Capt. J.F.P. Hamilton. Wounded Lts M.O. Roberts and J.L. Workman. 159
" 27th	In trenches in GHELUVELT. Fairly quiet day. The Chateau, gardens, and village were shelled.	Killed Cap. R.F. Balfour
" 28th	In trenches at GHELUVELT. Receive warning from our intelligence that Germans XXVII Reserve have been brought up and will attack at 5.30 a.m. tomorrow.	L/S R.H. Fitzroy and 2/Lt Sterling Short joined Battalion
" 29th	In trenches at GHELUVELT. Attack commenced punctually at 5.30 a.m. on North front. Heavy execution done by C and L.F. At about 12 noon the line on the East side of the Cross roads on the YPRES road, held by the Gloucesters, is broken and the Gloucesters and Black Watch are successively rolled up and retire. RF, & LC and 2 Coys of C.O. are thus isolated	Killed L. Sir A. Ogilvy Br. Wounded (Capt.) W.H.L. Stephenson (died of wounds) Capt. Sir H.E. Mackenzie Bt. 2/ Lieut G.E.H. Macdonald (missing) Missing Capt. CE. de la Pasture Lt. B. Gibbolitt C.F. Campbell H. Fitzroy

RF, & LC

Army Form C. 2118.

WAR DIARY
or
INTELLIGENCE SUMMARY.
(Erase heading not required.)

Hour, Date, Place	Summary of Events and Information	Remarks and References to Appendices
	and surrounded and nothing more heard of them. 2 Lieutenant T.C.O. and ⅔ of LF are thought to be killed which the hits of stragglers collected by Capt Segrave held enemy off all day and accounted for many Germans. 3rd Brigade is brought up in the evening and line re-adjusted	
Oct 30th	Heavy shelling. Enemys infantry had retired out of sight, but the woods E of GHELUVELT are full of them. The SW Borderers and now on our L and then Welsh and Queens across MENIN road.	
Oct 31st	The day commenced with very heavy shelling of the 7th Brigade. About 11 am the Welsh and Queens give. Soon after 2 Bn SW Borderers retired, and 2 LF brought up to reinforce line, but every advance along MENIN road and recovered GHELUVELT village. An hour later 2 Rn Worcesters Regt made counter attack and drove enemy out of Chateau garden here to wood. At 4 pm retirement ordered to new line 1000 yds in rear which was carried out unmolested	Killed Col W.S. McNair Wounded Major B.G. Vanderneyer (Engineers) 1 J.J.

 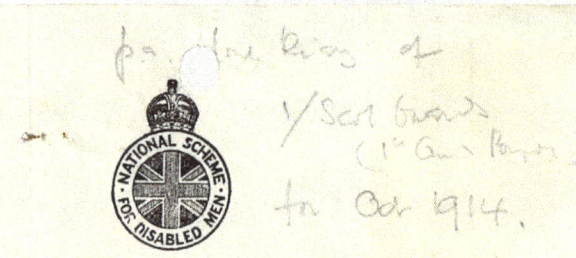

pa. for king of
1/Scots Guards
(1st Guards Brigade)
for Oct 1914.

HISTORICAL SECTION (MILITARY BRANCH),
COMMITTEE OF IMPERIAL DEFENCE,
2, CAVENDISH SQUARE. W.1.

20/9/21

(1) Did the British occupy BIXCHOOTE on 22nd October 1914, or did the Scots Guards hold the line near STEENSTRAATE? (The Germans say they evacuated BIXCHOOTE on the night of 22nd-23rd October by mistake

(2) Or,--- were the French troops in BIXCHOOTE on 22nd October 1914 when the Scots Guards arrived there ?

(3) Or,--- Did the Scots Guards turn the Germans out of BIXCHOOTE, or did they merely occupy the place ?

Dear Victor

Can you throw any light on the above? As he has not had his Diaries. I was with the 2nd Batt.n as B.M. to the 20th Brigade. The 2nd B.n were in Polygon Wood & Kruseik Ridge on these dates.

yrs M S Salis

Sept 22. 21.

BRACKLEY,
BALLATER,
N.B.

23-9-21.

My dear Colonel

Reference Enclosed :-

1. We held the line near Steenstraate & did not occupy Bixchoote or try to do so.
The Germans may have evacuated Bixchoote on the night of 22nd Oct. but I do not think so. They certainly re-occupied it almost at once if they ever left it, as I remember

our patrols getting in touch with attack whilst the trench were actually taken in that village, & they attacked relieving us, which we had to difficulty as to the Cameron's on our right in beating back.

On my front the 23rd or 24th Oct. Whether the trench actually held from the direction of Bixschoote Bixschoote before we arrived to

2. Some French Territorials came up

I eventually relieved us at ? (think) on the 24th. But they certainly were not in Bixschoote when we arrived at the former place. Incidentally the Germans made a feint-attack

Toft

Whether the French actually held Bixschoote before we arrived to afterwards, I cannot say — but think not.

G. Eyre
Vice le Actg?

Telegrams: "GUARDHOUSE, SOWEST", LONDON.
Telephone 2845 VICTORIA.

HEADQUARTERS,
SCOTS GUARDS,
BUCKINGHAM GATE, S.W.

Sept 27th/21

Dear Fergusson

I had to communicate with Victor Mackenzie about your letter. He was with our 1st Battⁿ. I enclose his letter in answer to your questions.

Yrs sincerely
[signature]

1st Guards Brigade.

1st Guards Brigade.

1st BATTALION

THE SCOTS GUARDS

NOVEMBER 1 9 1 4

Army Form C. 2118.

WAR DIARY
or
INTELLIGENCE SUMMARY.
(Erase heading not required.)

Hour, Date, Place	Summary of Events and Information	Remarks and References to Appendices
Nov. 1st	Trenches between VELDHOEK and GHELUVELT. Dug new trenches during the night - Fairly quiet day. Gloucesters on our right. In the evening Col. Churche Miller and two men Gloucester took men from Gloucester and 4th Dragoons across MENIN road - the 2/KRR on their right	1. S. G.
Nov. 2nd	Very heavy shelling. Hurricade destroyed. Gloucesters and KRR driven back. Enemy advanced down MENIN road and opened with machine guns at our rear and also enfilade artillery fire. C Coy driven back to go to Lee road Line reoccupied in the evening 300 yds in rear	Wounded, Lt. Sir I. Colquhoun Bt.
Nov. 3rd	VELDHOEK. New line consisted of a Bn of Zouaves and L.N. Lancs on MENIN Rd. Scots Gds, Camerons, Black Watch. Dig new trenches during night	
Nov. 4th	Quiet day. Huge round d'apres near wood round trench farm house	
Nov 5th	Heavy shelling	4th Reinforcement Sgt. Howson and 50 R and F.

Army Form C. 2118.

WAR DIARY
or
INTELLIGENCE SUMMARY.
(Erase heading not required.)

Instructions regarding War Diaries and Intelligence Summaries are contained in F.S. Regs., Part II. and the Staff Manual respectively. Title pages will be prepared in manuscript.

Hour, Date, Place	Summary of Events and Information	Remarks and References to Appendices
Nov. 6th VELTHOEK.	Fairly quiet day	9th Reinforcement 1/s 3 W.Smith, 60 R. and F.
" 7th — do —	Heavy Shelling.	
" 8th — do —	Heavy shelling. Enemy break through French and N.Lancs. got into communication trench and enfilade Battalion trenches. L.N.Lancs and our supports counter-attacked and regained lost trenches. Germans remained in right trenches. Attempts made to turn them out with machine gun fire.	Killed Lt R.N.Gipps Lt F.A. Monckton Wounded Lt. C.B.W.Smith (slight wounds) 1st Lt S.Spoor Lt.S.J.S.Dyer B₃ Missing Lt. A.W. Douglas Dick 1 S.P.
" 9th VELTHOEK.	Fairly quiet day.	
" 10th — do —	Heavy Shelling.	
" 11th — do —	Terrific shelling commencing at 6.30 a.m. and lasting for 3 hours. All trenches and dug-outs were knocked in. The Prussian guard attacked through VELTHOEK and took the front trenches along the whole of 1st Brigade. Our men in crowds hid in all trenches on either side were occupied by the enemy, and his good seventeen Prussian Guards were killed to pieces early in the morning and then attacked by infantry from the wood

WAR DIARY
or
INTELLIGENCE SUMMARY.
(Erase heading not required.)

Army Form C. 2118.

15

Hour, Date, Place	Summary of Events and Information	Remarks and References to Appendices
Nov 12th	Only 5 men from the fire trench so from the Orchard & from Point d'appui and Batt. H.Qrs. escaped and managed to rejoin rest of Brigade at dusk. Enemy got within 200 yards of our guns, he were driven back losing very heavily	S L
13th	The 1st Brigade went back to HOOGE in reserve – Capt Stracey and by R. F Scots Gds Capt Fortune and 109 men Black Watch Col McEwen Major Craig Brown & Dunderville and 140 men Cameron 1 Hrs. made dugouts in wood opposite HOOGE Chateau	
13rd	In dug. outs	
14th	Moved over to N. side of road and made new dug-outs	
15th	Snow and rain. The whole place a sea of mud.	Total Casualties in the YPRES District Killed Wounded Missing Officers 9 7 5 Other ranks 105 151 430
16th	Left HOOGE and marched via VLAMERTINGHE to WESTOUTRE, and billeted there. Lt Col Lowther C.V.O. C.M.G. D.S.O. rejoined & resumed Command.	

W A R   D I A R Y

Copied from first page of War Diary for December.

1st Scots Guards November 1914

Nov.17th	Marched to BORRE near HAZEBROUCK and went into billets for rest and refitment remaining there until December 20th.
" 28th	Battalion inspected by F.M. the Commander in Chief, Sir J.French G.C.B. etc.

5th Reinforcement (18.11.14
Major A.V.Poynter D.S.O
2nd Lts.Hon R.Coke,
H.G.Hill Trevor, Hon
R.Norton and 89 R and F

7th Reinforcement (29.11.14
2nd Lt.Hon.R.Bethell &
R.Dormer and 100 R and F.

1st Guards Brigade.

1st Division.

1st BATTALION

THE SCOTS GUARDS

DECEMBER 1 9 1 1 4

WAR DIARY or INTELLIGENCE SUMMARY.

Army Form C. 2118.

16

Hour, Date, Place	Summary of Events and Information	Remarks and References to Appendices
Nov 17th	Marched to BORRE near HAZEBROUCK and went into billets for rest and refitment remaining there until Dec 20th	6th Reinforcement (18-11-14) Major A.V. Payne DSO, 2nd Lts Hon. R. Coke, H.G. Hill Trevor, Hon. R. Norton and 59 Rank F. 7th Reinforcement (29.11.14) 2nd Lt Hon R. Bertrell and R. Dormer and 100 Rank F.
Nov 28th	Battalion inspected by FM the Commander in Chief Sir J. French GCB &c	8th Reinforcement (3-12-14) Lt A.G. Menzies and 100 Rank F.
Dec 3rd	Battalion with remainder of 1st Brigade inspected by His Majesty the King	
Dec 6th	Major Hon W.P. Hore Ruthven DSO arrived and assumed command of the Battalion	Cpl V.A. Orr Ewing joined 10/12/14
Dec 20th	Received orders at 1pm to be ready to move at once. Paraded at 4.30 pm and marched via MERVILLE to BETHUNE. Arrived at BETHUNE at about 2am 21st - Men dead beat after a march of 12 miles with driving rain. Battalion billeted in the girls' school. —	1.5.9
Dec. 21st	March off at 12 noon - BETHUNE - LA BASSEE Road. Turned N. at Cuinchy-Les-La Bassée and halt S. of Canal	

WAR DIARY or INTELLIGENCE SUMMARY

Army Form C. 2118.

Hour, Date, Place	Summary of Events and Information	Remarks and References to Appendices
	Opposite to three German trenches and establish ourselves in old trenches at Rue D'ouvert. Continued on right N. of Canal to GIVENCHY then Cameron Hrs Graham Gds Londonwich Black Watch (reserve). Heavy shelling across canal. Attack began at 4.15 A.M. and took up position N of GIVENCHY.	Killed Lt. A.G. Hill Tresor.
Dec. 22nd	R.F. B and C Coys in trenches 100 yds S of S.E. end of GIVENCHY village. L.F. about 200 yds in rear in reserve in dugouts. Nothing of any consequence. Very little shelling. Enemies opened fire at 5 p.m. to 9 p.m. back to CUINCHY, relieved by Munster Rgt (6th Bde). Two Companies relieved French at factory by canal (R.F. and L.F.) At 10 p.m. company ordered to go out and report junction between Black Watch and 3rd Brigade, as Munster Fusiliers whereabouts unknown	1 S.G.
Dec. 23rd	B Co go out at 10.15 p.m. at 1 a.m. told we might have to send more at 2 a.m. The C.O. and Brigadier went off to reconnoitre and found out what was happening. They ascertained that gap had been filled so they all return at 4 a.m. Billeted at CUINCHY 1 mile W of LA BASSEE on Canal. Village in lots been habitable in places. 2 Coys in trenches where dugouts were. Lt. Dormer posted to R.F. to take command temporarily. The Br was in Brigade reserve tonight and machine gun have gone back to Black Watch to relieve London Scottish. Quiet night.	

WAR DIARY or **INTELLIGENCE SUMMARY.**

(Erase heading not required.)

Army Form C. 2118.

Hour, Date, Place	Summary of Events and Information	Remarks and References to Appendices
Dec 24th	Billeted at CUINCHY. Men occupied in cleaning rifles and billets. Our machine gun relieved - they had two shoots (a) At a party of 20 early morning knocked over 6 - range 800 yards, and (b) in the Evening knocked over a bugler and some men when it froze, cold night.	
25th	At 7pm right half battalion went off to trenches at a farm and N.W. of it, in the N. side of GIVENCHY village. A bad place - some of the men having to be in the farm building (nightly shelled) and the trench in prolongation of is very narrow and shallow. No casualties during evening.	I.S.F
26th	Companies improved trenches. Left ½ Bn. relieved Right ½ Bn at 7pm. The pair animals took up 16 boxes of ammunition and lit them at the farm. 1 pair animal was hit in the stomach and had to be shot on reaching billets. Relief carried out without any trouble.	
27th	Trenches improved and dug in front of farm. Left ½ Bn. rg Cavallies Capt Anthony Wade was sent So Major Luthren took his place. No casualties.	

Army Form C. 2118.

WAR DIARY
or
INTELLIGENCE SUMMARY.
(Erase heading not required.)

Hour, Date, Place	Summary of Events and Information	Remarks and References to Appendices
Dec 28th	Relieved at 4 P.M. by Black Watch. Battalion marched back to BETHUNE. For a few days' rest. Men billeted in an orphanage and officers in a small chateau. Both very comfortable.	
" 29th-30th	In Billets at Bethune	I.S.Y.
" 31st	Orders received at 4.30 p.m. Moved off at 5 p.m. The Battalion had been celebrating near approach of New Year and several men had to be left behind.) Halted in BEUVRY for an hour then on to billets near CUINCHY at 10 p.m. Soon after arrival there 1 Company with ricks 8 & 3 sections was ordered up to CUINCHY Village. It appears that in the afternoon the KRR (2nd Bde) had lost an observation post and machine gun emplacement on Railway embankment and were about to attempt to re-take it. Our Coy was required to dig in as soon as road was recovered. Attack failed and Company was not required. At 11.30 p.m. orders were received for whole battalion to proceed to H.Qrs. of 6oth in CUINCHY at once. We were there informed that we were to relieve Munsters in all Coys moved up communication	2nd Reinforcement consisting of 2/Lt Monkton and 200 R and F.

1ST DIVISION
1ST BRIGADE

1ST BATTALION

SCOTS GUARDS

JAN - JULY 1915

1st Division
1st Bde.

WAR DIARY

1st SCOTS GUARDS.

January

1915

1915.
Jan. 1st

(qui) from previous month

War Diary

We were there informed that we were to evacuate position at all costs. There was no communication

2° Reinforcement
Capt S. Thorpe
Lt G.V.F Hooten and
20 R+

Colonel Thorpe
wounded

Army Form C. 2118.

20

WAR DIARY
or
INTELLIGENCE SUMMARY.
(Erase heading not required.)

Hour, Date, Place	Summary of Events and Information	Remarks and References to Appendices
	Trenches and dugouts on open ground 400 yards from entrenchment in 3 lines – 1st C Co. Capt Tracey, 2nd & Co. Capt Orr Ewing – 3rd R.F. 2nd Lt Dorner. L.F. with Gurkhas & Co. under Lt Hon: R. Legge in reserve. Advance well led by Capt Tracey. Commenced at 3 a.m. and by 3.30 am re-inforced by L.F. had captured the position. Once in the entrenchment the battalion came under heavy fire from Right and Left, and right rear – this last proving specially trying and causing many casualties. Officers holding on for over an hour it became obvious that the position was untenable and the battalion gradually withdrew to original position of deployment. 65 men under Lt Hon A Bethell remained in trenches until 6 p.m. when they were relieved by a similar number under the Adjutant	Killed Capt R.F. Tracey Lt. A.G. Menzies Wounded Capt N.A. Orr Ewing D.S.O 2Lt. R.S. Dorner
Jan 2nd	Trenches in very bad state, especially the Communication trenches which in places was over one's knees in mud. Trenches were made and bottom of trenches supplied with bricks and straw. Very cold. About 4 a.m. and heavy rain at 6 a.m. Good deal of sniping but no casualties. About 3.30 p.m. a shell burst in billets during rifle inspection wounding 10 men	Capt A.P. Kingsmill 2nd Lt. A.H. Long R. A Bell Smith # Creed (Gren.Gds) Joined for duty.

WAR DIARY
or
INTELLIGENCE SUMMARY.
(Erase heading not required.)

Army Form C. 2118.

21

Hour, Date, Place	Summary of Events and Information	Remarks and References to Appendices
Jan. 3rd	Battalion comes entirely under 10th Brigade and our men in trenches are relieved by the Essex Regt.	Major Buckworth was joined
" 4th	A, B and C and 1 platoon of D Coy go up to the trenches under Capt. Thorpe. "A" in reserve. "B" (under Long) of 200 yds. with detached posts in centre in trench close to river then about 60 men in trench "C" (with ---) in reserve then 20 men level with the other. 30 trenches in awful state, half falling in and communication trenches in places 3 ft of mud. Remainder of Battalion remain as 2nd line in Distillery.	S.F
" 5th	At 5 p.m. Distillery party relieve men in trenches except for 30 men in trench near Canal, who have to remain 48 hours. A number to relieve is not sufficient. Capt. Thorpe stays on as he, Romilly has touch of fever	
" 6th	Quiet as before	
" 7th	Very wet and trench falls in a good deal. Very little sniping as we shoot anything in sight. Quiet as before.	

WAR DIARY
or
INTELLIGENCE SUMMARY.
(Erase heading not required.)

Army Form C. 2118.

22

Hour, Date, Place	Summary of Events and Information	Remarks and References to Appendices
Jan 8th	Tremendous British bombardment of German trenches from 12 noon to 1 p.m. Relief as before. Wet most of the day.	
" 9th	Relief party starting at 5 p.m. took fascines and hurdles mid them to put in front of trenches. Relief (under Rafts) completed at 7.55 p.m.	2nd Lts. J. Denny and G.H. Fletcher (B. Coy) joined for duty
" 10th	Terrific British bombardment at 1.40 p.m. for about 1 hour. 142 guns firing and all neighbouring trenches assisting with rifle fire. It was about the biggest bombardment of the war and the whole ground seemed alive with shell. The Scots Regt attacked entrenchment where there was nothing living left and moved on to it without casualties.	S.P.
" 11th	Relief as usual. Quiet day.	
" 12th	Shelling early - going about 200 yds over. At 2.20 p.m. Germans started bombardment. Lively hour on our right along Canal. Minenwerfer bomb came within 60 yds of our canal trench. Two or three black Marias missed our river by 10 yards. Quiet at 5 p.m. Relief without difficulty at 7 p.m.	10th Reinforcement 2 Lt. G.E.V. Critchley and 29 R. and 5.

Army Form C. 2118.

23

WAR DIARY
or
INTELLIGENCE SUMMARY.
(Erase heading not required.)

Instructions regarding War Diaries and Intelligence Summaries are contained in F. S. Regs., Part II. and the Staff Manual respectively. Title pages will be prepared in manuscript.

Hour, Date, Place	Summary of Events and Information	Remarks and References to Appendices
Jan 13th	Quiet day. Relieved by Munster Fusiliers. Marched to BEUVRY and billeted. Last party got in about midnight	
" 14th	Left BEUVRY at 2.30pm and marched to BETHUNE for a while and. Billeted in École Michelin.	1.58
" 15th	BETHUNE. Cleaning up and refitting.	
" 16th	— " —	
" 17th	— " —	
" 18th	— " — The A.D.M.S. inspected the billets.	
" 19th	— " —	
" 20th	— " — Maj. Genl. Watkins Comdg 1st Divn. inspected billets.	
" 21st	Left BETHUNE and marched to billets at ANNEQUIN being inspected en route by G.O.C. 1st Corps - find in line and then in towns.	1st Reinforcement. Maj A.C.Morrison Bell, 2nd Lt A. Hammersley and 160 R. and F.
" 22nd	ANNEQUIN in billets. Route march, fatigue party digging trenches etc.	

(9 29 6) W 3332—1107 103,000 10/13 HWV Forms/C. 2118/10.

Army Form C. 2118.

WAR DIARY
or
INTELLIGENCE SUMMARY.
(Erase heading not required.)

Instructions regarding War Diaries and Intelligence Summaries are contained in F. S. Regs., Part II. and the Staff Manual respectively. Title pages will be prepared in manuscript.

Hour, Date, Place	Summary of Events and Information	Remarks and References to Appendices
Jan: 23rd	Left ANNEQUIN at 3.30 p.m. for trenches at CUINCHY. B and C Coys in fire trench. RF in "Keep". LF in reserve. Trench very close to Germans (25 to 150 yds) Our right hand men touching Lys Hand Frenchman	1 S F
" 24th	RF and LF take over fire trenches at 2.30 p.m. B C in "Keep". C in reserve.	
" 25th	At 6.30 a.m. a German deserter reported that an attack was going to be made on 2 our trenches. Information went first [and then] our trenches were to be blown in by [previously] made mines. After an hour all [reports] as Deserter had said. S RF and 40 LF got away - Their story is as follows - The Germans first shelled them, then got out of their trenches and attacked half right and shot down into the trenches. The Germans afterwards swarmed up to the "Keep" where Major Romilly was there they were checked and [the] Reinforcements came up and a counter attack was delivered at 1 p.m. but did not retake much ground. Battalion was relieved at 4 p.m. by Sussex Regt.	Killed Lt. H.S.E. Burg (8 Gds. attached) Wounded 2/Lt J.A. Denny (—) Missing Major A.C. Momssen Bell Lt G.V.F. Monckton Lt G.E.V. Gurteley 2/Lt A.H. Long (8 Gds. attached) 2/Lt G.H. Fletcher 2/Lt J.C. Thompson (Arriss Rifles attached) 2/Lt H.E. Weld (")
" 26th	Marched back to BETHUNE, battalion billeted in the Caserne Montmorency. till 2nd Feb.	Total Casualties in the CUINCHY (LA BASSEE) district Killed Wounded Missing Officers 4 3 7 Other ranks 27 120 235

2/2/15 LEFT BETHUNE → AUBIGNY

1st Division
1st Bde.

WAR DIARY

1st SCOTS GUARDS.

February

1915

Army Form C. 2118.

WAR DIARY
or
INTELLIGENCE SUMMARY.
(Erase heading not required.)

Instructions regarding War Diaries and Intelligence Summaries are contained in F. S. Regs., Part II. and the Staff Manual respectively. Title pages will be prepared in manuscript.

Hour, Date, Place	Summary of Events and Information	Remarks and References to Appendices
Feb 2nd	Left BETHUNE and marched to BURBURE (nr LILLERS) to billets for rest and refitment	12th Reinforcement (10.2.15) 2nd Lts J.A. Drury-Lowe and L. Norman and 200 R. and F.
Feb 2nd - 26th	Billets at BURBURE	Maj Lord Rosse, 2nd Lts D. Parsons and R. Rankin (Irish Gds) joined for duty (16.2.15)
" 27th	Left BURBURE and marched to OBLINGHEM	
" 28th	Left Billets at OBLINGHEM and marched to RUE DE L'EPINETTE for duty in trenches N. of FESTUBERT. Battalion in billets in reserve	
March 1st	In billets - reserve	
" 2nd	Relieved Cameron Hrs in trenches	13th Reinforcement (2.3.15) Lt E.P. OmManney and 150 R.&F.
" 3rd	Trenches	
" 4th	From trenches to billets in reserve	
" 5th	In billets - Reserve	

1st Division
1st Bde.

WAR DIARY

1st SCOTS GUARDS.

March

1915

Copy.

1st Scots Guards   March 1915.

1st Reinforcements (2.3.15)
2 ⟋ Lt CP Pott Leaving + 150 NCOs

March 1st   In billets - Reserve.
2d   Relieved Cameron Hrs. in Trenches
3d   Trenches.
4th   From trenches to billets, in reserve.
6th   In billets - Reserve.

WAR DIARY
or
INTELLIGENCE SUMMARY.
(Erase heading not required.)

Army Form C. 2118.

Instructions regarding War Diaries and Intelligence Summaries are contained in F. S. Regs., Part II. and the Staff Manual respectively. Title pages will be prepared in manuscript.

Hour, Date, Place	Summary of Events and Information	Remarks and References to Appendices
March 6th	Relieved Cameron Hrs in trenches	
7th	Trenches	
8th	From trenches to billets in reserve	
9th	In billets - Reserve	
10th	Heavy bombardment of the enemy's line by whole of 1st army artillery. Battalion in reserve all day. To move at short notice. Received orders at 5 p.m. to move off 5.45 p.m. towards RICHEBOURG L'AVOUÉ in support of Indian Brigade. Halted in roadside about 1 kilometre from RICHEBOURG until 11 p.m. and then received orders to return to billets at RUE DE L'EPINETTE. Arrived in billets shortly after midnight.	1st Reinforcement (9.3.15) Lt E.D. Mackenzie and 91 Rank F. Major B.H.S. Romilly DSO and A Kingsmill (Glas) wounded. 9.15 F
11th	Relieved Cameron Hrs in trenches	
12th	In trenches. Shell struck Batt H.Qrs about 7.30 a.m. wounding 4 signallers. Considerable shelling all day of H.Q village.	
13th	Quiet day in trenches. H.Q. village shelled. Good work done by Cpl. Frerier and Colins who volunteered to go out as patrols to German trenches to find out if held.	

WAR DIARY or INTELLIGENCE SUMMARY

Army Form C. 2118.

(Erase heading not required.)

Hour, Date, Place	Summary of Events and Information	Remarks and References to Appendices
March 14th	Relieved by Camerons & pc in trenches. Lt Col Fox Wiltshire Cdg 7th Bde reported Battalion & assumed command	
15th	In bivouac. Reserve. O'Reilly and self rode over at 11am where officers were at lunch - but no one else touched. Germans started shelling again with 6" shells as 5.30pm, the shells at 2 min interval pitching in field 100 yds at back of HQ. Lasted till 2.30am began again at 9am till 2.20am	
16th	Relieved Camerons &pc in trenches. Batt. HQ moved 300 yds along road S. of Bonnes place	
17th	In trenches	
18th	From trenches. 3 shells fell within 100 yds of Br H.Q	1st R. improved (9.3.5) Lt Sir J.S. Dyer and 30 R and Z
19th	In Billets. Reserve	
20th	Relieved Camerons &pc in trenches	
21st	In trenches	

Army Form C. 2118.

28

WAR DIARY
or
INTELLIGENCE SUMMARY.
(Erase heading not required.)

Instructions regarding War Diaries and Intelligence Summaries are contained in F. S. Regs., Part II. and the Staff Manual respectively. Title pages will be prepared in manuscript.

Hour, Date, Place	Summary of Events and Information	Remarks and References to Appendices
March 22nd	Battalion relieved by Northampton Regiment and Companies returned independently to BÉTHUNE and billeted in Collége des jeunes filles	Total Casualties in RUE DE L'ÉPINETTE district. Killed Wounded Missing Officers – 2 – Other Ranks 12 40 –
" 23rd	Remained at BÉTHUNE	
" 24th	Paraded at 8.20 a.m. and marched to TOMBE WILLOT near LOCON where battalion billeted in scattered [farm houses]	S.E.
" 25th – 29th	At TOMBE WILLOT resting.	
" 30th	Left TOMBE WILLOT, the right ½ Bn. proceeded to VIELLE at LE TOURET and the left ½ Bn. to RICHEBOURG ST VAAST Battalion in brigade reserve. M. Guns in trenches under Brigade arrangements	2nd Lts Ambrose and C.O. Bay Richebourg joined Battn.
April 1st – 2nd	Brigade Reserve	
" 3rd	Took over trenches from Gloucester Regt & Relief completed by 11 p.m. Wet night	
" 4th	In trenches "A" Coy, 21st Bn London Regt. attached to Battn. – a platoon to each company. Rain in night. Trenches 18" deep	
" 5th	Quiet day. Rain in night. Trenches 18" deep in water in places.	

1st Infantry Brigade.
1st Division.

WAR DIARY

1st SCOTS GUARDS.

APRIL

1915

On His Majesty's Service.

1 Kings Own

War Diary

1914

April 1st - 2nd   Brigade Reservr

3d   Took over trenches from platoon Gds. Relief completed by 11pm. Wet night.

4th   In trenches. "A" Coy 21st Bn London Regt attached to 1st — a platoon to each Company.

5th   Quiet day. Rain at night. Trenches 18" deep in water in places.

WAR DIARY
or
INTELLIGENCE SUMMARY.
(Erase heading not required.)

Army Form C. 2118.

Hour, Date, Place	Summary of Events and Information	Remarks and References to Appendices
Ypres 6th	Tomorrow to go to trenches as a complete company. Kept carrier pet in Ypres.	2Lt C. Bartholomew Joined Bn?
7th	In Trenches. Bad sniper there & prisoners on the last 4 days.	
8th	In Trenches	
9th	— do —	
10th	— do —	
	Support trenches shelled in afternoon	
11th	Went up supporting Battalion relieved by Cameron Highrs. Relief began at 7.30 pm completed at 10 pm — Batt HQuarters and Left ½ Bn at LE TOURET - right ½ Bn RICHEBOURG ST VAAST	Total Casualties in RICHEBOURG ST VAAST district Killed Wounded Missing Officers 9 — — Other Ranks 9 28 —
12th - 14th	Battalion in Brigade Reserve	
15th - 23rd	Battalion in Divisional Reserve at TOMBE WILLOT Company Sports held in Billets	16-4-15 1st Reinforcement Capt E. Mapleton, 2Lt N. Ferguson 2nd 100 Rank?
22nd	Battalion on RUE DU BOIS hurrying ups Off Billets	18-4-15 1st Reinforcement Capt J.H. Gibson DSO, 2nd Lt Heart H.?
	at 6 pm Turned Tex. ys S of West H.Qs	Meiresen and 23 Rank?
	at 8 pm - dig all 11.30 pm and got their about	23-4-15 Lt Hon M Howard 1875
	2 am — What invested in diggings 216 Trucks putting	5 Bn?
	in Cable and filling up again	

Army Form C. 2118.

WAR DIARY
INTELLIGENCE SUMMARY.
(Erase heading not required.)

1/ Scots Gds. 30

Instructions regarding War Diaries and Intelligence Summaries are contained in F. S. Regs., Part II. and the Staff Manual respectively. Title pages will be prepared in manuscript.

Hour, Date, Place	Summary of Events and Information	Remarks and References to Appendices
April 24th	Paraded at 5.20 pm and marched to Rue de Lannoy, GONNEHEM, about 4 miles and go into billets. Army/Corps Reserve.	25.4.15 18th Reinforcement Maj. A V Payn- 250 and 50 RxF 27.4.15 19th Reinforcement 70 R and F.
25th Apl	GONNEHEM - Corps Reserve	

1st Infantry Brigade.
1st Division.

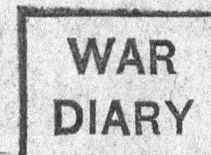

1st SCOTS GUARDS.

MAY

1915

On His Majesty's Service.

1st Scots Guards.
May 1915.

			Casualties:	
			Killed	Wounded

May	1st	Gonnehem	Fighting strength C.O. and Adj., 16 Coy Officers, 862 other ranks. Machine Guns 29 machine-gunners. 21 signallers and orderlies; 13 pioneers; 5 snipers; and 4 trench-mortarmen available for trenches.		
"	2nd		Paraded at 4.30 p.m. to relieve 5th Sussex in D3. Rue-du-Bois. Route N13.O.Y Cannot, Pont Levis – Locon, Locouture and Windy Corner. Arrived Windy Corner at 8 p.m.		
"	3rd		During the morning the Germans shelled the supply trenches considerably and also put several bombs into the front trenches. The bombarded their trenches with 6" and 9.2" for about 20 mins. Line near killed. D3. 4mm from the Cinder track bankwork about 450 yds. Very good trenchworks with good parados.	1	7
"	4th	Trenches D3.	Very quiet. Think a German relief we cannot cut last night as new late(?) very quiet. Germans shelled Rue du Bois in the afternoon. No damage. Relieved by Coldstreams beginning at 9.15 p.m. completed 11.30 p.m. We had to find fatigue party of 3 Officers and 300 men. "B" Coy billeted the night at Richebourg.	1	5
			– do –		

Army Form C. 2118.

WAR DIARY or INTELLIGENCE SUMMARY.

(Erase heading not required.)

Hour, Date, Place	Summary of Events and Information	Remarks and References to Appendices
May 5th	Inspection of Billets. Instruction from Brigadier regarding forthcoming attack	
" 6th.	Recon. ground over which Battn. would have to advance. Very quiet save very little shelling.	
" 7th.	At Richebourg	
" 8th.	Richebourg - Quiet day. Complete preparation for tomorrow attack. Battn. marched off at 9.30 pm to position of assembly. Order of march - Reg.ts "R.F." "B" "C" "L.F." Rifle half Battn. and Coys in farms on Rue de Bervais. Left half Battn. ½ mile N. on Windy Corner Richebourg Road. Fairly dry but cold and uncomfortable night.	
" 9th.	Bombardment commenced 5 am. At 5.40 Battn. moved forwards to occupy trenches in line C behind houses on North side Rue du Bois. Moved on artillery formation across ½ mile between position of assembly and Rue du Bois. On the failure of the assault by 2st and 5th Brigades, Coldstreams and Black Watch, ordered to occupy front line of trenches while in and Coldstreams sent back and took cover in 2nd line. We sent "B" and "L.F." coys. fwd to 2nd assault in afternoon. Regt. on withdrawn and billeted at Hinges. Very fine day.	Casualties:— Wounded— Colo. Pelham, Capts. G. Westmacott sent back from A.P. Station all by little Gen. Willert - Sgt. Garroway 5 R and F. Wounded 3 + 45.
" 10th.	Hinges - Very Good billets. March in afternoon to Les Harisoits. Very fine.	
" 11th.	Les-Harisoits - Billets. Scarce. Received orders to relieve Irish Guards at Givenchy tomorrow. Very fine.	

Army Form C. 2118.

32.

WAR DIARY
or
INTELLIGENCE SUMMARY.
(Erase heading not required.)

Instructions regarding War Diaries and Intelligence Summaries are contained in F. S. Regs., Part II. and the Staff Manual respectively. Title pages will be prepared in manuscript.

Hour, Date, Place		Summary of Events and Information	Remarks and References to Appendices
May 12th		Battn. left Harrisoirs 9.45 am. Marched through Hinges (left transport) to Bethune. H.Q.A. here to dinner. 1.45pm on march again for Givenchy. Relieved Irish Guards in trenches in front of village "R.F." and "B" in front lines; "C" in support, "L.F." in reserve. Very few guns and scarcely ½batth. Quiet night. Fine to cloudy.	
"	13th	In trenches – Quiet day. Known shelling by Germans but little damage done. 5.30 pm received order that Regts. would probably be relieved tonight. 7.15 pm Received orders Battn. to be relieved by London Irish. Relief not complete until next morning. Very wet. 1 o'clock permeated by our artillery. Battn. marched back to Rithing (?) captains among to coys of Bethune in theatre and skating Rink. Fine.	
"	14th		
"	15th	Bethune – Received orders to relieve 2/5th French Regt. at Le Rutoire, nr Vermelles. Quiet night, raining	
"	16th	In trenches – Germans shelled trenches and knocked out one of our machine guns. Fine	Casualties – Killed; Wounded 1 2
"	17th	– do – Quiet day. Some shelling by Germans. Very wet.	– do – 3
"	18th	– do – Considerable shelling of our trenches by Germans. Cold and wet.	– do – 2
"	19th	– do – Germans continue to shell our trenches. Relieved by 1st Coldstreams, and marched back to Sailly Labourse. Fine.	– do – 4

Army Form C. 2118.

33

WAR DIARY
or
INTELLIGENCE SUMMARY.
(Erase heading not required.)

Instructions regarding War Diaries and Intelligence Summaries are contained in F.S. Regs., Part II. and the Staff Manual respectively. Title pages will be prepared in manuscript.

Hour, Date, Place	Summary of Events and Information	Remarks and References to Appendices
May 20th	Sailly Labourse — In Billets. Moderate, rather scattered. Large fatigue parties at night for digging. Weather fine.	
" 21st	— do — Digging parties at night. Showery	
" 22nd	— do — — do — Thunderstorm at night.	
" 23rd	— do —	
" 24th	Relieved 1st Coldstream at Le Rutoire. "C" and "L.F." Coys. reliefs at 4 p.m.; remainder of Battn. at 7.30 p.m. Quiet night. Fine.	
" 25th	In Trenches — Quiet day. Very fine.	
" 26th	— do — Quiet day, but some shelling in evening by Germans. Very high. Casualties — Wounded 4	Wounded 4
	3.50 p.m. Broke on our right German heavy bombardment of German trenches, ceased 4.20 p.m. No attack made and no reply on our trenches except rifle on French.	
" 27th	— do — Relieved by 1st Coldstream. In Brigade Reserve. "C" "L.F." and Hqrs. at Noyelles. "R.F." and "B" at Vermelles. Fairly good Billets.	— do — Killed 1 Wounded 1
" 28th	In Billets at Noyelles and Vermelles. Fine.	
" 29th	— do —	
" 30th	— do — Some shelling by Germans to damage done. Stray from Church	
" 31st	In Billets at Noyelles and Vermelles. Some shelling by Germans. No damage done.	C.O. Acting appointment as C.S.I. 27th Div. 31/5/15

1st Infantry Brigade.
1st Division.

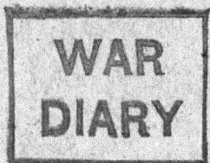

1st SCOTS GUARDS.

J U N E

1915

On His Majesty's Service.

Army Form C. 2118.

34.

WAR DIARY
or
INTELLIGENCE SUMMARY.
(Erase heading not required.)

Instructions regarding War Diaries and Intelligence Summaries are contained in F. S. Regs., Part II. and the Staff Manual respectively. Title pages will be prepared in manuscript.

Hour, Date, Place	Summary of Events and Information	Remarks and References to Appendices
June 1st.	In Billets at Noyelles and Vermelles. 11am Lt. Col. The Master of Rutheven left Bours. to take up appt. as G.S.I. 47th Div. Capt. Fir Victor Mackenzie Bt. takes over command of Battn. relieved by 7th London (Post Office Rifles) and go into billets at Beuvre also Jeanne Pillers. Bethune. Very fine.	
" " 2nd.	In Billets at Bethune. Inspection of Billets by C.O. Very fine.	
" " 3rd.	In Billets at Bethune. Very fine.	
" " 4th.	— do —	
" " 5th.	In Billets at Bethune. Battalion inspection by G.O.C. 1st. Corps. (Genl. Monro). Bathing Parade. Very fine.	
" " 6th.	In Billets at Bethune. Church Parade. Very fine.	
" " 7th.	In Billets at Bethune. Washing Parade and Bathing Parade. Very fine.	
" " 8th.	In Billets at Bethune. Thunderstorm	
" " 9th.	— do — Thunderstorm	Very materially damaged whole in billets however
" " 10th.	In Billets at Bethune. Lt. Col. Holman arrived and assumed command of the Battalion. Bathing and washing. Relieved 1/5 Notts Derbys in trenches in country sector. "R.F." "B" and L.F. Coys in firing line; "C" Coy in support.	Casualties:- 3 killed

WAR DIARY or INTELLIGENCE SUMMARY.

Army Form C. 2118.

35.

(Erase heading not required.)

Instructions regarding War Diaries and Intelligence Summaries are contained in F. S. Regs., Part II. and the Staff Manual respectively. Title pages will be prepared in manuscript.

Hour, Date, Place	Summary of Events and Information	Remarks and References to Appendices
		Casualties
		Killed / Wounded
June 11th.	In Trenches at Cambrin. Bombing over shelling by Germans.	
" 12th.	— do — Some shelling by Germans.	1 / 3
" 13th.	— do —	3 / 12
	"R.F." to Cambrin. "B" and "C" Coys in close support at Cuinchy.	
	"L.F." in dug outs just east of Cambrin.	
" 14th.	At Cambrin. Village shelled by Germans.	2
" 15th.	— do —	1 / 6
" 16th.	— do — Weather fine	1 / 3
	Received Orders to proceed to Labeuvrière on relief by 1/2 R. Lancs.	
" 17th.	At Labeuvrière. C.O. inspected fire	
" 18th.	— do —	
" 19th.	— do — Coy. training, etc. fine	
" 20th.	— do —	
" 21st.	Voluntary Church Parade. fine	
" 22nd.	— do — Coy. training, etc. cricket match "L.F." v. "R.F." Won by "C" Coy.	
" 23rd.	— do — Cricket match "L.F." v. "R.F." Won by "L.F." Thunderstorm	
	— do — "L.F." v. "C" Coy. Won by "L.F." Raining	
" 24th.	Battn. moved into billets at Pontrue. 10 am. another from Battn. fire	
	Labeuvrière 1.3.5 amunition Ruethenne Billets timed.	

Army Form C. 2118.

36.

WAR DIARY
or
INTELLIGENCE SUMMARY

(Erase heading not required.)

Instructions regarding War Diaries and Intelligence
Summaries are contained in F. S. Regs., Part II.
and the Staff Manual respectively. Title pages
will be prepared in manuscript.

Hour, Date, Place	Summary of Events and Information	Remarks and References to Appendices
June. 25th.	At Bourbre. Coy. engaged in cleaning up Billets. Football match between Oannon Coy. and Batn. took place in afternoon. Result: Draw, 1 goal each.	
" 26th	At Bourbre.	
" 27th	- do - Voluntary church parade.	
" 28th	- do - Company practice attacking with bombs on training ground. Rates Boxing Tournament in afternoon.	
" 29th	Battalion marched to VERQUIN. Very hot day and a large number of men fell out. Billets very crowded.	
" 30th	At VERQUIN. 2/Lt. Bartholomew and Lt. Hon. Jones returned from leave.	

1st Infantry Brigade.
1st Division.

WAR DIARY

1st SCOTS GUARDS.

J U L Y

1 9 1 5
(1.7.15 - 3.8.15)

1st Scots Guards.

July 1915

July 1st.	At VERQUIN	Companies employed on various their occupations. Football match in evening between "B" and "L.F." Coy. Won by "B" 2-1 goal to nil
2nd	- do -	Companies practice attacking with bombs. Lt- Browne gone to field Ambulance injured by one of the bombs.
3rd	- do -	Batt. match employed on fatigues. Football match in afternoon between Battn. and Canadians. Won by Battn. - 1 goal to nil. Very hot.

On His Majesty's Service.

1st Scots Guards.

July 1915

July 1st	At VERQUIN	Companies carrying under their commanders. Football match in evening between "B" and "L.F." Coy. Won by "B" 2 goals to nil
2nd	do	Companies practice attacking with bombs. Lt. Browne gone to Field Ambulance injured by one of the bombs.
3rd	do	Bn. mostly employed on fatigues. Football match in afternoon between Battn. and Canadians. Won by Battn. - 1 goal to nil. Very hot.

Army Form C. 2118.

37.

WAR DIARY
or
INTELLIGENCE SUMMARY

(Erase heading not required.)

Instructions regarding War Diaries and Intelligence Summaries are contained in F. S. Regs., Part II. and the Staff Manual respectively. Title pages will be prepared in manuscript.

Hour, Date, Place		Summary of Events and Information	Remarks and References to Appendices
July 4th	At VERQUIN.	Three German shells fell in village. 4 men of R.F. very badly wounded. Very hot day.	
" 5th	- do -	2/Lt. Thompson returned from leave. Marched to the Future and attached 1/S.W. Borderers in trenches. Very fine.	
" 6th	In trenches at LE RUTOIRE.	"B" and "C" in front line "L.F." in support "R.F." in reserve. Quiet day fine. Casualties - Nil	Casualties. Killed. Wounded. 1 2
7th	- do -	- do -	
8th	- do -	Quiet day, fine.	
9th	- do -	Quiet up to 7 p.m. Germans shelled new front line with H.E. shell.	Nil.
10th	At LABOURSE.	Relieved by 1/Coldstream guards and went into Brigade reserve billets at LABOURSE. Finis. 2/6. Norman and Ferguson return from leave.	
11th	- do -	Church Parade. C.O., 2nd in command O.S.C. Coys. made reconnaissance of new defensive line.	
12th	- do -	Relieved 1/Coldstream guards at LE RUTOIRE.	

WAR DIARY
or
INTELLIGENCE SUMMARY
(Erase heading not required.)

Army Form C. 2118
38

Instructions regarding War Diaries and Intelligence Summaries are contained in F. S. Regs., Part II. and the Staff Manual respectively. Title pages will be prepared in manuscript.

Hour, Date, Place	Summary of Events and Information	Remarks and References to Appendices
July 13th	In trenches at LE RUTOIRE. Quiet	
14th	— do —	
15th	— do —	
16th	— do — Relieved by Coldstream Guards and went into billets at VERMELLES	
17th	At VERMELLES. Village shelled in morning.	1 wounded (afternoon event major)
18th	— do — Quiet.	
19th	— do — Relieved by 2nd K.R.R.C. at 10.30 p.m. and proceeded to VERQUIN took over billets from 1/L.N.Lancs.	
20th	At VERQUIN.	
21st	— do — "B" and "C" Coys musketry on range	
22nd	— do — Bathing at Bethune. Football match Bn. v. Camerons in afternoon. Won by Camerons 4 goals to 1	
23rd	— do — "R.F." and "L.F." musketry on range	
24th	— do — Brigade Horse show at Champs two splits ANNEZIN. Battn won 3 firsts, 2 seconds :— Machine gun limber } 1st Light Draft Horses } Water cart	S.A.A. cart Officer jumping comp. } 2nd

(9 26 6) W 257—976 100,000 4/12 H W V 79/3298

Army Form C. 2118.

WAR DIARY
or
INTELLIGENCE SUMMARY
(Erase heading not required.)

39.

Hour, Date, Place		Summary of Events and Information	Remarks and References to Appendices
July 25th	At VERQUIN	Relieved 1/Plymouth Regt in Z.2 South of LA BASSEE road "R.F" "B" and "C" in firing line; "L.F." in support.	
26th		In trenches at Z.2	Casualties Wounded 1
27th		— do —	
28th		— do —	Killed 1; wounded 6
29th		Relieved by 1/Coldstream Guards and went into Billets at SAILLY LABOURSE	
30th		In Billets at SAILLY LABOURSE — Large dugout parties at VERMELLES	
31st		— do —	
August 1st		— do — Relieved 1/Coldstream Guards in Z.2 just South of LA BASSEE Road. "L.F." "R.F." over "B" in firing line and "C" Coy. in support	Killed 1
2nd		In trenches South of LA BASSEE road. Some bombing by enemy, which ceased on our artillery firing.	Movements Capt J.H.Cuthbert 2/i/c slightly wounded. Remains on duty.
3rd	In trenches	Much bombing during night by enemy which was silenced by own artillery. 2/Lt. E.J.B. Boyd - Rochfort finished up a live enemy bomb and threw it over the parapet. Relieved by 1/Coldstream Guards and went into Billets at SAILLY LABOURSE	Wounded 1
	— do — (Z.2)		